# NEARLY There

## A COLLECTION OF POEMS BY

# MICHAEL TOD

Michael Tod was born in Dorset in 1937 and lived near Weymouth until his family moved to a hill farm in Wales when he was eleven. His childhood experiences on the Dorset coast and in the Welsh mountains have given him a deep love and knowledge of wild creatures and the countryside, which is reflected in many of these poems and in his Squirrel, Dolphin and Elephant novels.

At the time of the publication of this volume Michael is in his 82nd year. He now has three grown up children, three grown up grandchildren and two great grandchildren and still writes the occasional poem. This book may be considered as his swansong.

Other books by Michael Tod

*The Silver Tide*
*The Second Wave*
*The Golden Flight*
Novels with squirrel characters. Now available in a single
volume –    *The Dorset Squirrels*

*Dolphinsong* – A novel with human and dolphin characters.

*God's Elephants* – A novel with human and elephant
characters.

*Barefoot Summer* – three short stories set in Wales.

*The Ferry Boat – Finding a Credible God.* Non-fiction

Copyright in the contents of *Nearly There* is waived by the
author.

*Nearly There* and all of the above named books are available
for down-loading as Ebooks.

Published by Cadno Books 2018
Cadnobooks.co.uk
michaeltod@btinternet.com

ISBN 9781898225089

# Nearly There

by

## Michael Tod

*In a poet's wood*
*All the trees are of crystal*
*He can hide nowhere.*

Lim Do Tchae.

This book is dedicated to the memory of
my friend and fellow poet
Barbara Anne Knight
(1944 – 2017)
whose poem *November Wood* contains the perceptive line
'Fragile as happiness'

The whole of her poem *November Wood*
is reproduced in this volume on Page 73.

Acknowledgements.

Cover illustration – Debbie Devauden
Cover photograph – Des Pugh
Photograph page (iii) – David John

I would like to thank other people who helped me develop what skills I have in composing poetry, notably Catherine Merriman and the late Keith Evans. Also those who have helped in the production of *Nearly There*, especially Judith Keeling for copy editing and Mike Brown for technical assistance in preparing the manuscript for publication.

Thank you all.

# Introduction.

I hold very strong views on the writing of poetry. The first is that a poem should be complete in itself and need no separate introduction. I do get cross if I attend a reading and the poet spends as much time explaining about the meaning or the setting of the poem before it is read, as it takes to read the poem!

If the poet needs to do this, I believe that they have not spent enough time on the poem and are wasting *your* time and mental energy. To write a worthwhile poem takes skill, time and effort, which should be spent by the poet themselves so as to make *your* hearing or reading of the poem crisp and concise.

The second of my 'rules' is that the message of the poem should be accessible at the first reading or hearing. There may well be deeper, less obvious meanings hidden in the text that may develop or emerge with re-reading but the fundamental meaning should be clear at the first experience.

Having said all this, the poem Gypsy Mary (page 46) does need a little elaboration now. At the time I wrote this in 1989, most people who were likely to read it would have remembered my mother, Dorothy Elizabeth Tod, known to generations of scouts and guides as 'Cap'. One of the kindest and most loving people I have ever known, she trusted everyone to be as honest and straightforward as she was. I inherited this naivety and it has often cost me dear!

*Michael Tod*
*Abergavenny,*
*September 2018.*

## KERNELS OF TRUTH / MYKU

A Kernel of Truth is based on the Japanese 'Haiku' verse form. The Haiku consists of seventeen syllables arranged in three lines, with the first and third lines having exactly five and the middle line having exactly seven syllables. There is no requirement for the lines to rhyme. There are several other rules for the verse to be a true Haiku, such as the need for at least one word to indicate the season of the year.

I first came across a haiku many years ago when I saw the film *The Wind Cannot Read.* The story was set in Japan in the period immediately after the Second World War. A young army officer, who was part of the American occupying force, was allocated a beautiful Japanese woman as his official translator. Regulations forbade any socialising with the ex-enemy. Inevitably the couple fall in love.

The opening sequence of the film showed a park with tulips in bloom and a sign reading 'Do not pick the flowers'. The camera moves in to a close-up shot of the petals being blown away and a voice-over says

> *The sign in the park*
> *Says 'Do not pick the flowers'–*
> *But the wind cannot read.*

Without knowing this was a Haiku, or even knowing that such a verse form existed, I was moved by the by the power and beauty of the verse and remembered it for some thirty years before starting to write poetry myself.

I simplified this concept when I was writing my novel *The Dorset Squirrels,* so that the squirrel characters lived by Kernels of Truth which were taught to them when they were youngsters. A typical squirrel Kernel would be –

> *One out of eight nuts*
> *Must be left to germinate*
> *Here grows our future.*

*Squirrels without aims*
*Drift through life, vulnerable*
*To each passing whim.*

*If you think you can*
*Or if you think you cannot –*
*Either way you're right.*

Over the years I found this format to be an excellent way to capture ideas and express them poetically. I continued to use the title 'Kernels of Truth' and many of these were published in my earlier poetry book, *A Curlew's Cry*, in a subsection *A Bag of Mixed Kernels*. In *Nearly There* they are scattered among the other poems.

Kernels of Truth seemed a clumsy title and was inappropriately long for a verse whose essence was concise brevity. Yet to call them Haiku would offend those who expect the verse to comply with all of the appropriate rules. Hence I created a portmanteau word – Myku combining the possessive *word My with the latter part of Haiku. Myku are* essentially personal and should impart the writer's own view of the subject.

If you should wish –
*To write a Myku,*
*Find, distil, encapsulate*
*A thought that moves you.*

Myku do not have titles. The scene must be set within the tiny verse itself and it is important that each Myku contains the entire meaning of the verse, even when it forms a part of a poem made up entirely of Myku as in *A Night Long Remembered*. (Page 34)

*A Myku cannot*
*Be quoted out of context.*
*Each one is complete*

Myku can be used to make a wry point –

> *Punctuality*
> *Goes unappreciated.*
> *Nobody is there.*

They can be used to paint a scene –

> *A girl on a swing.*
> *Skirt billowing in the wind.*
> *Such joy on her face!*

Or they can be used to pass on a wise saying –

> *If you are lucky*
> *And have a whole loaf. Sell half*
> *And buy a lily.*

Or they can make a tongue-in-cheek comment such as –

> *Migrating seabirds*
> *Don't fly alone. One good tern*
> *Deserves another.*

I hope that you enjoy the selection of Myku in this book.

An Index of TITLES and first lines will be found on pages 75-79. Myku are identified by the first line being set in italics.

# A CURLEW'S CRY

Hearing a distant curlew's bubbling cry
My heart with hiraeth fills
This sad, lonely sound distils
Sun and wind on Wales' hills.

Hireath – a welsh word meaning an intense longing to be home.

----◇----

# DEBBIE'S SONG

At Ely, in the fens of Cambridgeshire,
There stands a great cathedral on a hill
And here I set my scene.

Some half a century ago, my young and lovely wife
Wheeled our first-born daughter
In her high, white pram in through the western door.

When right beneath the famous lantern tower,
Sitting in her pram, bright eyed and rosy cheeked
Debbie began to sing.
No words, she was just six months old,
But such a song of joy all other visitors
Stood where they were and listened quietly.

Debbie sang on
Enchanted by the echoes of her voice
Coming from all around
And from the lantern tower high above.

When her song was done,
She clapped her little hands in joy.
The other folk, silent 'til then,
Applauded too.

I wish I had been there
But often now I visualise that magic scene
And smile with love.

----◇----

1

A KINDLY WORD

**A pie, a pint and a kindly word –
Five pounds'**, the menu read.
But the girl who brought my pie and my pint,
Well – never a word she said.

I handed her a five pound note.
'Where's the kindly word?' says I.
She glanced behind her, lowered her voice
And said, *'Don't eat the pie!'*

----◇----

BOYHOOD      Part One: Rhythms of the Sea.

When I was born the sunlit, sparkling sea
Patterned the ceiling, light delighting me.
And, as I grew, that sea was always near,
Gull's cries and wave sounds ever in my ear.
Barefoot amongst the worm-casts on the rippled sand
I wandered free, my little body tanned
By salty breezes that the grown-ups shun,
My child's eyes narrowed by a hazy sun
That warms the pools bait-diggers leave behind.
A seagull feather was a special find
Held high, vibrating in my hand
Then thrown aloft to spin towards the land,
Forgotten in a moment; something new
Would catch my eye: a bright green copper screw,
Sand-polished glass, a cork, a piece of wood,
Cuttlefish bones or whelk's eggs, each was good
To handle, smell, abandon  -  half a minute's joy  -
Each common thing a treasure to this little boy.

I learned the run of currents, times of tides,
I knew the sandbar where the flatfish hides,
I'd find the oyster-catcher's hidden nest
Amongst the flotsam. Their alarm made manifest
Through plaintive piping, tricks with broken wings
Decoying me away.  But other things
Along the high tide mark would catch my eye,
A driftwood dragon, seaweed crisp and dry,                >>>>

2

(My favourite was many-bubbled bladderwrack,)
Pinching each black balloon to make it crack)
Dead guillemots, striped Brasso tins
From Naval ships, dried dogfish with sandpaper skins
And soggy sailors-hats blown overboard.
Such riches - I'd collect a hoard
And leave them on the beach, run home for tea,
Tomorrow would bring more in from the sea.

Then there were boats - learning to row and sail -
My brother's voice: "Don't let the painter trail."
The skill of skulling with a single oar,
The thrill of landing on an unknown shore
Across the bay, to sleep beneath the sky,
Only a sail to keep the bedding dry.
Rising at dawn to catch an off-shore breeze,
Watching for catspaws, grey on sunlit seas,
Feeling the ropes as stiff as rods, the canvas taut,
Heeling with gunwale dipping, braced against a thwart.
Then sudden calm, bow-wave and bubbling wake subside
To drift in silence on the morning tide.
Alert for eddies warning 'sunken rocks'
We'd drift along.  We had no clocks,
The angle of the sun, the rate of flow,
Sounds from the land, the way the seabirds go,
Told us the hour.  So were these early years to me –
A life in tune with tides and subtle rhythms of the sea.

----◇----

BOYHOOD     Part Two: Cwm Cadno Days

When I was ten, we left that magic coast:
The lovely hills of Wales were to host
My adolescence. There upon a hillside farm
I grew to manhood. There I learned the charm
Of misty valleys seen from high above,
The croak of ravens, cry of curlews, coo of dove.
To wake to mooing as the cows came in,
Rattle of buckets, bark of cowman's dog, the din
Of milking time, muted by distance, penetrating sleep.
Breakfast of porridge, pile into the Jeep
And down the hill, churns clanking on the back, to school.

>>>>

3

That was an alien place to be. I'd play the fool
And waste the time I spent there - that was me -
To be indoors was living purgatory.

I loved to shoot. I learned the marksman's skill
And many a rabbit shot, (though now I never kill)
I'd track the foxes' paw-prints in the snow
To find a stillborn lamb, eyes taken by a crow,
Then back to join the others on the sledge,
Fly down the meadow, crash into the hedge,
Shouting and laughing in the frost-still air;
The world was somewhere else – we had no care.

On summer evenings we would go to swim
Down to the Usk, then watch the swallows skim
The water where migrating elvers swam.
Sometimes in mountain streams we'd build a dam
With stones and turf and moss to make our pool
Then wallow naked in the water cool.
How innocent we were with simple joys,
All Wales for our playground – lucky boys!

----◇----

BOYHOOD     Part Three: Scouting

But it was scouting that I loved the best,
Tracking and hiking, passing every test
To win my badges. Learn the woodsman's lore,
Tree-felling, cabin-building, use of axe and saw.
Master my knots, throw bridges over streams,
Climbing, canoeing, caving – many schemes
Of high adventure filled each holiday.
The summer camp when we would go away
To Exmoor, western Wales or Wareham Heath
Set up our tents and sleep beneath
A canvas roof. To wake to pigeons in the pines,
Crawl from warm beds to make bee-lines
Through grass and bracken to a smelly loo.
A trail of footprints in the morning dew.

Breakfast was eaten standing in the chill
Before the sun had cleared the eastern hill.
Blue-rimmed enamel plates piled high with beans,
That staple base of many camp cuisines,
With smoky stews, burnt custard, soggy duff,
To hungry boys it all was good enough
For *we* had cooked it, called it 'lovely grub'.

Wide-games we played through woods and scrub.
Built gadgets out of sticks and string,
Devices that would hold just anything
And keep our campsite smart. Then after dark
We'd gather round a campfire; put a spark
To birch-bark tinder, well dried logs. There in the glow,
Our favourite songs we'd sing with more gusto
Than melody. In sun or rain each joy-filled day would pass,
Fond memories now, mere shadows on the grass.

----◇----

BOYHOOD     Part Four: Apprenticeship

At sixteen years I was apprentice-bound.
A job at Seargeant Brothers had been found,
To suit my aspirations to create
Beautiful things  –  Bookbinding thought appropriate.
I learned to fold and sew the pages of a book
And work with glue and paste, but never overlook
The need to keep the workbench clean, and free
From sticky splashes, lest the foreman see
And castigate this 'mucky lad' – the boy
He had to train and teach that loving joy
A real craftsman had in all he did and made.

Leather was good to handle, every shade
Of colour held. Many a different skin,
Stiff vellum, glossy basil, skivers thin
I had to learn to work with. Cut with care,
Softened and folded, rubbed down on a pair
Of covers, spines then bound with cords
And clamped into a press between two boards.

>>>>

I loved, and feared, the power guillotine,
Its heavy blade, honed razor keen,
Sheared stacks of paper with a single stroke.
For me, though safely guarded, how it would invoke
A fear of fingers lost. But big old Bill
Who worked this dread machine, had still
All those he had been born with, but it was his joke
To keep two folded down and tell new folk
Joining the firm, how they had been chopped off –
Elaborating blood and gore, then scoff
When they felt faint and moved away.
Bill loved this little joke, it made his day.

I also learned the way to form a gel
For marbling paper, boiling seaweed well,
Letting the extract set, and on the top,
In random patterns, colours drop.
Tradition specified red, blue and black
Followed by ox-gall, pushing back
The colours, making marble veins.
Lay on the paper, taking pains
To get no bubbles. When it was quite smooth
Lift by one corner, carefully remove
The paper, hang it on a line –
Each sheet unique, an individual design.

Sometimes I worked with leaves of gold
Beaten so thin that, if I lost my hold
The leaf would float on air, as light
(Though made of metal) as a feather might.
The gold was melted with a heated tool
To block-print titles which, when cool,
Would not rub off, but glowed
Impressed in leather, never to corrode.

On special books we used these leaves of gold
To gild the edge of pages. In a press we'd hold
The sheets clamped tight together, then with white
Of egg, we'd paint the surface – lay the gold on right,
Then burnish with an agate. Thus I learned my trade.

I wonder now: where are those books I made?

----◇----

BOYHOOD    Part Five        An End to All of This

I know you'd like to hear about the girls
I courted then, who, when and where. These pearls
Of memories are safe inside my private shell
And not for sharing. So I'll never tell
Of furtive fumblings, cuddles in the hay,
Walks by the river. I will not betray
The secret pleasures while we learned how we
Were different from one another, he from she!
School 'Social Evenings', playing 'Postman's Knock',
Shy kisses. Home by ten o'clock!

Dear Fanny Jones's vain attempts to teach
Me how to dance  -  she would beseech
Me, towering above, to move my feet
In time with something that she called 'the beat'
That I was deaf to. In the end
She gave up trying. She is still my friend.

Mr. Medina, living down below the farm
Befriended me. With his so easy charm
His cine-camera he would lend to me.
In my imagination I would be
A great director filming epics grand.
With cardboard megaphone I'd stand
And call directions to a cast of scouts
And my dog, Reddy, who'd ignore my shouts.
Bribing with titbits was the only way
To get co-operation in our play.

In those days, colour film was rare
So we used black and white. Our Premiere
Had plink-plonk music from a tape machine.
Invited guests to see us on the screen.
So amateur, no Oscars would be won
But making it, we had a lot of fun!

Boats and the sea, hills and the farm, being a scout
Bookbinding, courting, making films – without
Much in the way of future plans – a jolly game....

My boyhood ended when my Call-up Papers came.

----◇----

## PLAIN JANE

The young men called her plain and went their way.
"It's pretty girls we want," I heard one say.
But, once, I saw the love-light in her eyes,
And Jane, though plain, was beautiful that day.

----◇----

*Rainbows, kingfishers*
*And happiness – don't stay long.*
*Each a fleeting joy.*

----◇----

## HAREBELLS

In chapel as a child
I found a harebell, heavenly blue,
Pressed in my hymn book.
How long it had been there
I didn't know. The flower
Was thinner than the pages
Which had crushed it flat.
It was still bright
And smelt of mountains.

Towering above me,
Stern, unsmiling faces,
Dark serge suits,
Another sombre Sunday.

Dust drifted golden in the sunbeams.
Moses' rod and water gushing in the wilderness
Suddenly seemed a minor miracle
To what I knew was happening –
Outside.

Slipping unnoticed
Past the giant trousered legs,
I left.

>>>>

"I like the atmosphere," I said,
"Excitement, bustle, city life, pub chatter.
London has everything!
Theatres, galleries,
Writers and artists,
History and pageantry."
What more could I desire?

Yet, in my bedsit
I could not recall a show I'd seen,
Meeting a real writer,
Seeing a picture that I could compare
With Mynydd Pen-y-Fal from Skirrid Fawr,
Harebells around my feet.

Slipping unnoticed
Past the giant tower blocks
I left.

----◇----

*It is a pity*
*That Noah could not resist*
*A unicorn steak.*

----◇----

LARKS AND OWLS

Some men and women (of which I am one),
Rise early and are instantly awake
But energy sinks with the setting sun.
We 'larks' quite quickly to our beds then take.

But other people, rising later on,
Are bright and active far into the night.
They only tire with the darkness gone,
The pseudonym of 'owls' would seem just right.

How odd that 'larks' and 'owls' are always wed,
I've often pondered on this strange affair.
They often quarrel when the other stays in bed.
Of Nature's purpose they are unaware.

>>>>

Nature evolved this process of selection
So 'man cubs', in the cave, had most protection.

----◇----

ONE GOOD CHURN

Two frogs fell in a bowl of cream
And started swimming round and round.
"There's no way out," the weak one said,
Gave up and sank and drowned.

The other frog, of sterner stuff,
"I won't give up," was heard to utter
And went on swimming round and round,
Then hopped out from the butter.

----◇----

*Migrating seabirds*
*Don't fly alone. One good tern*
*Deserves another.*

----◇----

SOME PEOPLE'S THOUGHTS

Some people's thoughts are sparkling mountain streams
Reflecting sunshine, shallow, bright and clear.
No need to search for depth, just passing  dreams,
Popular clichés splash and tinkle here.

Some people's thoughts are merely winterbournes
In 'summer good times' empty, dried-up bores,
Each sudden storm a raging flood then spawns
And passing, leaves just flattened grass and straws.

Some people's thoughts rush through a steep ravine,
Pitted with polished holes where stones go round,
Grinding great hollows where their souls have been.
Deep in dark pools, rare gemstones may be found.

>>>>

Such precious jewels should be keenly sought,
These adamantine relics of some poet's thought.

*(Winterbourne – a stream-bed empty in summer,*
*becoming a river in winter or during a storm.)*

----◇----

*You will be much loved.*
*No matter what else you lack.*
*If you are just kind.*

*If you are just kind.*
*No matter what else you lack,*
*You will be much loved*

----◇----

KISSING HANDS

Helen
When first I saw
Your baby hand, born fingerless,
I cried and put it to my lips
A vain attempt to 'kiss it better'.

Later I learned to kiss each hand
To show I didn't mind
And let you know that every part
Was just as precious as the rest.

Now, when I watch you play
Handling each problem with such joy and zest
I kiss your hand
From sheer respect

I never notice which.

----◇----

## HOBSON'S BUTTERFLY

Two caterpillars chomped along a leaf.
One hairy brown, one luminescent green.
Their life was one big munch – no grief
Disturbed this meal – their futures quite unseen.

A butterfly, tan, orange, red and black
Flew over, floating, tumbling in the breeze
Thrown upwards, downwards, sideways, forward, back,
Twisting and turning through the sunlit trees.

Said Luminescent Green to Hairy Brown,
"That creature's tossed by every wind that blows.
A faulty concept – wing design unsound –
You'd never get me up in one of those!"

----◇----

*True security*
*Comes from the acceptance of*
*Insecurity.*

----◇----

## MY HILL

They're going to build a wind-farm on my hill,
That hill I see across the valley now.
My hill.

They say I do not own my hill.
I have no title deeds, no legal right,
No valid interest in what they're going to do.

It's not enough to say I love that hill,
Have seen it in a thousand different moods,
Enjoyed for many years its peace, its calmness,
Its stability.

It's not enough to say I love to stand
And watch cloud shadows slide across its face
To say how I enjoy its dignity and majesty.

>>>>

12

I will admit to being green,
Fearing Chernobyl in this pleasant land
And I was one who thought the answer must
Be blowing in the wind.

But I have seen, since then, on other people's hills,
The lines of urgent, waving, drowning arms
That crowd their distant skies.

No more will 'jocund day
Stand tiptoe on my misty mountain top'.
Instead I'll see the flailing three-armed cross
On which my peace of mind is being crucified –
And cry.

----◇----

## A DROP OF DOGGEREL

I interviewed a man last night
Who'd just come up from Tooting.
Though blind from birth, his claim to fame
Was – he loved parachuting.

I asked him how he knew the time
To brace himself for landing.
He answered with a ready smile
At my not understanding.

"It's easy, Mike," the man replied,
"I have this simple knack.
I know when I am near the ground –
My guide-dog's lead goes slack".

----◇----

*Fear knocked at the door*
*Courage went to answer it*
*And no-one was there.*

----◇----

## CULTURE UNFATHOMED    (Written in 1994)

"They have no culture, they are savages."
Therefore we were quite free
To kill the men and use their women,
Corrupt their children,
Force them to fear our 'loving God'
And make them work the 'empty' lands for us.
Firearms imposed our will.

"They have no culture, they are only whales".
Therefore we are quite free
To hunt and kill, for oil and flesh
To feed our pets and gourmet Japanese.
Call it 'Research for Science',
Pretend it's for the good of Whales.
Harpoons impose our will.

Yet now we know the 'savages'
Did have a culture, different from ours,
In tune with Nature
And the places where they lived.
But it's too late – the last sad remnants fade,
Old men and women pass away to Dreamland,
Only rock paintings and their artefacts remain

A thousand years from now, if men exist,
Will they remember then
The gentle singing giants of the deep,
Whose culture we have failed to comprehend?
Our human brains inadequate,
Our intellects earthbound.

Instead we reach for Space.
It's there we hope to find intelligence
As great is ours.

----◇----

*Kingfishers flash by.*
*A glimpse of blue and orange.*
*Blink and they are gone.*

----◇----

14

# FROM WHENCE COMETH

I need the sight of hills.

They do not have to be the Himalayan 'Far Pavilions',
Though I would dearly love to stand
On Rhododendron-shaded trails and see
Those mighty mountains crowd the sky.

In Africa I saw Mount Kenya shyly flash
A glimpse of equatorial snows
At dawn and dusk,
And watched the rising sun glow pink on crater rims
At nineteen thousand feet.

I've photographed the peaks and glaciers
On Alps too perfect to be real
And learned it is not size that counts
For almost any modest hill will do.

How I survived two years at Ely
In the level fens, I do not know.
My eyes would scan the distant view
Making from clouds a fantasy
Of jumbled peaks and vaporous valleys.
Imagined mountains for an aching soul.

Now, when I turn mine eyes unto the hills
I see the Blorenge, Pen-y-Fal and Skirred Fawr.
No giants these
Yet help comes forth.

Familiar outlines fill a vacant space.
A pattern is complete within my mind.
I turn away and face the World
My inner strength restored.

I need the sight of hills.

----◇----

*In a long, rich life,*
*A high spot for me – climbing*
*Kilimanjaro.*

----◇----

15

# A NEST OF HORNETS

One summer we had hornets at the farm,
Yellow and brown, three times the size of wasps.
That know-all, Alan Pritchard, said,
"Their sting will kill a cart-horse."
Scared as I was, I vowed I would locate their nest,
And burn them out.

I saw myself a saviour – to my boyish mind
I'd be Saint George, slaying a fearsome foe.
Each evening I would try and trace the route
These dreaded creatures took,
But as they flew so fast, I always failed.

My brother Gareth found the answer.
With a tube of Balsawood Cement,
We glued a feather to a hornet's back
And followed it, unwitting Judas, to the nest.

Across the dingle, into Evan's Wood,
The feather led us, to a hollow oak
Where, as we watched, its bearer entered,
Followed by others, unadorned.
We trembled where we stood,
Thinking of all the cart-horse killers in the tree.

That night we came again
With tins of petrol and a light
And, greatly daring, poured it in the hole
Then struck a match and threw that in as well.

Standing well back, we heard the sullen roar
Of fire within the trunk consume the nest
And in the glow, watched late-returning workers
Flying in, get scorched and die.

We were the heroes of the hour.
I could not stay away,
Returning often in the following days
To watch the wisps of smoke
From smouldering punkwood rise,
Mixed with the ashes of a thousand virgin queens.

>>>>

16

Forty years on, I thought I saw a hornet in my wood.
I could be wrong, it might have been a wasp
Though late, in June, to see a queen.

I hope it was a hornet,
I would hate to know I was the human
Who had put the torch
To that last remnant of an ancient race
Whose right to life was just as great as mine.

----<>----

ARMISITICE PARADE AT ELY CATHEDRAL 1957

We stood, a hundred servicemen and girls
In uniforms of khaki and of Air Force blue
And in our midst a single sailor, home on leave –
One volunteer, at least.

In that huge, medieval nave
We sang 'O Valiant Hearts'
And heard the Padre tell
Of 'Pastures Green' and 'Death's Dark Vale'.
To honour those who fell,
In war, when we were children,
And in that other dreadful war
They called the 'Great'
Some thirty years before.

A bugle sounded from the gloom
Down by the Western Door
'The Last Post' – sombre, slow and sad –
Echoing.
Each heavy note,
Drifting among the pillars and the tombs
To fade away and die
In corners dark.

We heard the words,
Familiar to us all,
'Age shall not weary them,
Nor the years condemn'.

>>>>

Then – from that same simple instrument
Sprang forth 'Reveille'.
Notes of purest gold – lighting the gloom
Darted above our heads,
Soared up
Into the massive vault of Ely's Lantern Tower
To flutter there like doves
Drawing our souls up Heavenwards.
No death had been in vain!

There in my youthful innocence
I thought, 'If I should die
In some strange land,
I would not mind
If I could know
I would be remembered thus,
Each year
By bugle calls at 'Ely in the Fens'

And then we marched back
Through the driving rain to Camp.

----◇----

FEELING WELSH

I was just ten years old
When first I came to Wales
English by birth and parentage,
Of Scottish ancestry,
And even now I am betrayed by accent –
Vowels broad. 'Apples' and 'castle' are two words
Which label me a Dorset man. Yet I feel now
More Welsh than English.

The men of science tell
That water makes the greater part of us,
Ninety per cent or so.
If this is true, my body must be largely Welsh
From water drunk or bathed in.
Wales absorbed in liquid form?
But no, it isn't this
Or all the Brummies would feel Welsh as well!

>>>>

Is it the language then?
It can't be that.
I only have a smattering, enough
To translate names of places on a map.

Knowledge of history and legend?
No, the Mabinogion I cannot follow through.
Llewellyn and Glyndwr are little more than names.
And 'Modern Culture Wales'
Seems full of English-haters,
Poets filled with maudlin thoughts
Of mining dereliction and 'The Rape of Wales',
Or obscene ranters.

Can it be The Song?
I love to hear 'Myfanwy' but I cannot sing,
Have never heard a male voice choir in the flesh,
Though once I passed a well-known Rugby ground
And heard ten thousand singing Sospan Fach.

If there is something that has made me feel Welsh,
It must be hiding in the Hills.
An emanation from the ground absorbed when walking?
Something implanted in the ear
By skylarks, curlews, ravens, doves?
Patterns of skylines viewed,
Imprinted on the brain? Or scents –
Crushed bracken, soil steaming in the sun,
Or woodsmoke drifting on the evening breeze?
Tasted perhaps, in blackberries or mountain whins
Or water sipped at moss-draped springs
High up where sheep and rugged ponies graze?

The hills of Wales have subtly drugged and captured me
An Englishman,
Who feels Welsh.

----◇----

*It is more noble
To give a book, than lend one.
The cost is the same.*

----◇----

## MY DAFFODIL

One long past Spring I walked alone
Through gloomy woods along the riverside,
And there to my surprise and joy,
A single golden daffodil I spied.

Torn from its bed by winter's storms
And tossed upon the raging flood
Its bulb then cast upon the bank
To rot amongst the stones and mud.

The life inside would not be stilled
Though bruised and battered by the world,
But in that cold and hostile place
Its golden petals had unfurled.

Now daffodils may dance in hosts
And so delight some poet's eye,
But my brave, lonely daffodil
Will flower within me till I die.

----◇----

*If you are lucky*
*And have a whole loaf, sell half*
*And buy a lily.*

----◇----

## ADAM AND EVE IN ORBIT

Five, four, three, two, one.
Not "Blast off", just a gentle lift
From prototype Atomic Fusion motors.
Swiftly we climb, Professor Melanie and me,
Into Earth orbit.

When we look down,
The earth, a globe of green and blue,
Moves past our window –
So beautiful when seen from Space.

>>>>

We circle once, look down on Cape Canaveral,
It's gone!
A pool of magma, boiling rock,
Spreads outwards.

Someone has blundered –
A calculation not complete?
Computer error? Hell!
We stare aghast
And orbit on,
Remote spectators.

We circle twice.
Florida is boiling coast to coast,
The sea is steaming round a spreading ring.

Once more around
The Southern States and Mexico
Have gone.

Each orbit more destruction
At seventeen,
The icecaps melt
And we alone are living,
So far above what was the Earth –
Just Melanie and me.

How soon before the land can be repopulated,
Five, ten, twenty million years?
We haven't got that time,
Professor Melanie and me.

----<>----

PONDERING THE INFINITE

"Time always was and Time will always be,
And space goes on forever," I am told.
My mind can't grasp these concepts, they are far too big for me,
I try and form a picture, but the images won't hold.

>>>>

I can visualise a Decade and a Century as well
A Millennium is almost in my reach
But the idea of 'Eternity' just makes my mind rebel
And the thought breaks up and scatters like a shipwreck on a beach.

Primeval Man's evolving brain just didn't need to know
Of 'Time' beyond his threescore years and ten,
 And 'Distance' was a three day hunt, as far as he could go,
And then carry back his quarry to the den.

"Infinity – think on it," my puny brain I ask,
But the tool just isn't equal to the task.

----◇----

BLESS THIS HOUSE

Dusk in mid-afternoon
I raced the storm down from the sombre hills,
Hail rattling on my anorak.
Numb fingers fumbled with the mountain gate
Into a nettled yard.
Beyond it stood the house, stone roofed,
Unlived in now, but offering
Promise of shelter.

Blue painted door,
Tied with a bow of rotting binder-twine
To keep out sheep,
No barrier to me.

I stepped into the cobwebbed gloom
Of stone-flagged kitchen where,
Shivering,
I looked around.

A candle in a bottle,
Knobby with waxen drips,
Stood on a deal table.

>>>>

Lighting the wick,
I saw the unswept hearth,
A rug of knotted rags,
Thick with black dog hairs, dusty.
No sign of recent life.

Hung on a nail, a calendar
Gave me my clue.
Five years had gone
Since last a sheet had been torn off,
To show 'December 1965'.

Above the fireplace
A text, in darkwood frame,
Proclaimed that 'God is Love'.
Tucked in behind the frame,
A sprig of shrivelled holly leaves,
Berries black wrinkled currants now.

A model of an eager dog,
A minor trophy,
Tarnished, with peeling silver plate,
Was on the mantelshelf.

I took it in my hand and saw
A vision from the past –
A hillside in the sun,
Low whistle heard,
Intent black dog moves forward at the crouch,
A stick extends an outstretched arm.
Sheep penned, gate closed,
Grudging applause –
I gently put the trophy back upon the shelf.

I knew behind the corner door
I'd find a spiral stair
Within the thickness of the wall.

In flickering candlelight
I tiptoed up the worn stone steps.
A brass-knobbed bed half-filled a tiny room.
I was relieved to find no occupant.

>>>>

Though on the end a pair of trousers hung,
And mildewed boots stood, waiting, on the floor.

Above the bed another text said
'Bless This House'.

Going downstairs, I sensed the grief
Of dying alone at Christmas.
No woman there to tidy up,
No family to take the farm in hand.

How long before the dog, unwittingly,
Had told a neighbour of his master's death
By scavenging in hunger
At their door?

A shaft of amber sunlight lit the room
I stepped out, into clean-washed air,
Putting to flight a magpie from the yard,
And left the unblessed house

I hope God loved the shepherd.
I had seen no sign that others did –
Except,
Perhaps,
The dog.

----◇----

THE BUSHMAN'S TALE

A night in Africa.
Above – the stars hang bright.
Not far away a lion coughs and grunts.
A fire burns, lighting a ring of faces round about,
Making the velvet darkness darker still.

I was a guest,
My hosts a bushman family.
This desert was their home
And had been for a million years.
I sat among them and I heard this tale –

>>>>

*Once, long ago,*
*A hunter, drinking at a dawn-bright pool,*
*Saw the reflection of a great white bird,*
*But, when he raised his head,*
*The bird was gone.*

*He drank again, then rising*
*Followed to the north,*
*Leaving behind his home, his family,*
*The hunting grounds he knew so well –*
*All that was dear to him.*

*For years he searched in vain.*
*Then, old and weak,*
*He reached a cliff impossible to climb*
*But he was told that, at the top,*
*Was this bird's nest.*

*As he looked up,*
*A feather, white,*
*Came floating down*
*And landed in his hand.*
*He died there, on that rock,*
*Content.*

And here the story ended.
A woman threw a branch upon the fire.
Sparks flying upwards, twisted towards the stars.
I turned, a question on my lips –
"This bird," I asked. "What was it called?"

The wizened bushman who had told the tale, said,
"In our legends it has many names.
In all my dreams it is The Bird of Truth."

----<>----

*The scent of woodsmoke*
*Caught unexpectedly, stirs*
*Pleasant memories.*

----<>----

*A poet looks for –*
*Not just the bare facts but the*
*Underlying Truth*

*Poets just express*
*What other people feel – but*
*Can't articulate*

*Poets must express*
*What other people feel – but*
*Can't articulate*

----◇----

HANDS UP FOR A THIRD MILLENNIUM (Written in 1999)

Only the whales and dolphins have evolved
A bigger brain than ours
But we have hands –
Hands for manipulating tools,
For holding pens or brushes,
Instruments for saving life -
Or guns for taking it.

Forests of air-renewing trees
Scream with the bite of power saws.
We see on every hand
Quarries  and roads erode
Thyme-scented hills.

Oceans, at one time vibrant with the songs
Of many whales
Are handy sumps
To catch the effluents of affluence.

We cannot hand ten million beavers back
Their stolen skins
Retusk dead elephants
Rehorn a rotting rhino's skull…

>>>>

Recall how
In the *First* Millennium
People around the world took
Only what they needed then
To live from hand to mouth.

In the next
We let our arrogance and greed
Skin, scalp, eviscerate and poison this
So handsome planet – Earth.
And now, hands reaching out,
We race into a new millennium.

Slap, slap these grasping, errant hands of ours
And make us worthy of a Third.

----◇----

NOT ALWAYS BLACK – The Song of the Mynydd Ddu

*(The Black Mountains of South-East Wales.)*

The English call us '**black**'. Perhaps we seem that way,
When from a distance viewed, across the Wye,
But those who know our moods from day to day
Will say a name like that is just a lie.

In Spring and Summer we are many shades of green,
In Autumn, yellow, russet brown and gold,
In winter, often white with snow we're seen,
But '**black**' – well, sometimes – if the truth be told.

----◇----

*The Royal Air Force*
*Borrowed my life for six years.*
*Then gave it back.*

----◇----

*The longest distance*
*Walked between any two points*
*Is called a short cut.*

----◇----

27

*When work overwhelms,*
*A thousand things must be done –*
*Go climb a mountain.*

----◇----

A FLY IN AMBER

Ten million years ago a fly
Mistakenly
Landed on resin weeping from a wounded tree,
Was trapped and,
As the tree wept on,
Encapsulated,
Perfectly preserved.

Was this an ordinary fly
The same as others of its time?
We have no way to judge
For just this one
Was fossilised
I hold it here,
In amber
Perfectly preserved.

Ten million million words are uttered every day.
Which will survive the predators of time?
It may be those that have been trapped
When wounded mankind wept.

"Father, forgive them."
"Et tu, Brute?"
"To be or not to be."
"We'll fight them on the beaches."
Words like these
Will live on,
Perfectly preserved.

But who will make the final choice?
Which word or phrase
Will be the fly that only briefly flew,
But acts as representative,
Encapsulated,
Perfectly Preserved?                                    >>>>

28

If I could name a single phrase or word
That might survive ten million years,
Trapped in the amber wept by Man,
It would be: "While there's life, there's Hope"
Or simply
"Hope".
Either would do – if
Perfectly preserved.

----◇----

JANE'S PLATE

Below the Darren, where the ravens nest,
Half hidden in a sheltered dell,
A long abandoned shepherd's cottage stood
And here we children of Cwm Cadno played at 'house'.

Although the rooms were open to the sky
We didn't care, or even notice this.
We'd light a fire in the old stone hearth
For boiling hedge-laid eggs
And baking lumps of dough.

We called the long-dead shepherd Sam,
His wife was Jane, and sometimes we were they.
At other times we called ourselves their children,
Helping with lambing, shearing, making hay
And tying bags of raddle to the tup.

Poking around amongst the stones
As children do, I found a broken plate,
Well hidden in a secret place.
China so thin and delicate that,
When I held it up against the sun,
I saw the outline of my fingers clear
Though on the other side.

Porcelain patterned with flowers, red and blue,
Around the edge a ring of gleaming gold.
I held the pieces in my hand,
Enchanted.

>>>>

29

I was alone that day and,
Seated on a stone, holding the shards
I saw a scene so real
It must have been.

A child had taken down the plate
From off the dresser where it stood,
Jane's pride and joy, a wedding gift from Gran.
On climbing down, had slipped
And dropped the purloined treasure
To the floor.

The child and Jane were crying, Sam came in,
Tired and hungry from the hill.
He roughly took the pieces from Jane's hands
And threw them in the midden,
"Useless now."

The picture darkened. I saw Jane,
Holding a lantern, find the broken bits
And hide them in the place I'd found,
Out of Sam's sight.

I took the pieces home to show to Mam.
Megan, who knew about these things,
Or thought she did, said it was very old,
And rare, and had it been complete
Would have been worth
"A bob or two."

I kept them for a week,
Whilst I enjoyed the colour and the silky feel
Of antique porcelain, then took them back.
They still belonged to Jane.

Last year. I poked about, as adults do,
In Portobello Road
And found a plate, identical to Jane's.
But perfect, not a chip nor crack.
I bought it, though it cost
More than "a bob or two"
And took it home,
Safe in a padded box.

>>>>

30

Only the ravens know where it is now.
Today, when Mary asked
"Where is that plate you bought?"
I said, "it must be in the attic.
Look! There's a polly-wagtail on the lawn.
Look – over there."

----◇----

THE PAPER BOY

Pity the paper boy in Winter
Trudging the streets in pre-dawn darkness,
Sludge-splashed by passing cars,
Glimpses of families at breakfast
Remote in cosy kitchens.
Headlines all gloom and doom.
Pity the paper boy in Winter
Driven by greed, or need.

Envy the paper boy in Summer,
When sun lights up the quiet streets.
Cycling illicitly on pavements,
Watching the early birds,
Greeting the joggers.
How trivial the headlines now.
Envy the paper boy in Summer.
All this – and pocket-money, too.

----◇----

A PARADOX

From Lulworth Cove to Kimmeridge the Army owns the land,
And it's here that soldiers practice killing men.
For years they wired off the range, and you and I were banned
For only guns and tanks had access then.

From Kimmeridge to Lulworth Cove the Army was 'the boss'
And the only things to plough the ground were tanks.
The houses and the gardens were submerged in weeds and moss
And bracken, ferns and brambles hid the banks.

>>>>

From Lulworth Cove to Kimmeridge the Army's dropped its guard,
And, just sometimes, they will let the public through.
Here we marvel at the wildlife that abounds in every yard
Where no pesticides have poisoned with their soil-polluting brew.

In the battle for survival, should you be a caterpillar,
It's the Army who protects you, it's the farmer who's the killer.

----◇----

THE HUMAN CANNON-BALL

When Granville's Splendid Circus came to town,
It came with horses, elephants, a clown
And acts to hold the audience in thrall.
The best of these: 'The Human Canon-ball'.

A little  man was Jim, and round –
Trusty, reliable and sound.
He'd been with Old Man Granville many years.
To lose him was the least of Granville's fears.

Each night the drums would roll as Jim would climb
Into the cannon's mouth and in a second's time,
A bang, a cloud of smoke and Jim would jet
Across the ring, land safely in the net.

His fame was legion, people came
From far and near. Jim's other name –
'The Human Canon-Ball', brought special glory
To Granville's Circus – hence this little story.

A rival Circus Master – call him Ben –
Persuaded Jim to join him in the end
By offering a wage so sumptuous
That even loyal Jim could not refuse.

When Jim told Granville he was going soon
Granville said, "Pack up this afternoon.
I'm sorry you are leaving us behind,
Men of your calibre are hard to find".

----◇----

## THE ABACUS OF GOD

I stood upon the mighty Chesil Bank,
For mile on mile the sea-churned pebbles ground.
Each stone a boulder was before it sank
But waves and time have made them pebbles round.

Each man is born a sharp and jagged stone,
Life knocks the corners of us all, until
Into our own appointed place we're thrown
With others – yet an individual.

Perhaps it is a cosmic counting frame,
A pebble scores the life of each good man.
The Tally Roll of Heaven ~ in God's game,
A marker for each one who kept to plan?

It wasn't just a shingle beach I trod.
I stood upon the Abacus of God.

----<>----

*Be Kind, be Gentle*
*And be Fair. Three simple rules*
*To guide you through life.*

----<>----

*Successful people –*
*Those who get up one more time*
*Than they are knocked down.*

----<>----

*Punctuality*
*Goes unappreciated.*
*Nobody is there.*

----<>----

# A NIGHT LONG REMEMBERED.

The Mount of Olives
Night, woodsmoke on the warm breeze,
A peaceful place this.

Disciples near by
Laying on the stony soil
Talk amongst themselves.

"Watch and pray with me."
Jesus asks of them. In vain –
For, tired out, they sleep.

Jesus, restless, prays,
His back against a tree-trunk,
Hands in his lap now.

Lanterns prick darkness,
Muffled voices, clash of swords,
Soldiers are coming.

To betray Jesus,
False Judas chooses a kiss
The symbol of Love.

Swords strike, an ear bleeds.
"Who lives by the sword." Christ says
"Shall die by the sword."

Fear overcomes love.
Disciples scatter, run off,
Hide in the darkness.

From Gethsemene,
Mark, deserting his master,
Fleeing, runs naked.

"I'll not deny you."
Peter swears, meaning every word.
Then the dawn cock crows.

----◇----

# THE CHURCH BY THE LAKE

The wind of Spring was singing in the churchyard pines,
Wavelets were sparkling, dancing in the sun.
The heavy door swung open to my push.
Inside was silence.

In this house of God,
I prowled about,
Reading the tablets on the wall,
The Roll of Honour, names
Of men who left their lakeside homes to die.
The flowers from Sunday last
Fading and drooping here, today.

Near to the door, a book invited me:
PLEASE PRAY FOR THESE…
'A Mother, very ill.'
'A child dying of leukaemia.'
'People of Bosnia,
Sudan, Somalia.'
A catalogue of human grief.
Not praying, I read on,
My vision blurred,
'A son on drugs.'
'A missing daughter, gone from home
To God knows where.'

I closed the book
And turned to look along the quiet nave
To where a cross gleamed gold.

The heavy door swung open to my pull.

The wind of Spring was singing in the churchyard pines,
Wavelets were sparkling, dancing in the sun.
A mallard flew a cross across the sky,
Marsh marigolds heaped mounds of treasure round my feet.
A pair of swallows, following blind instinct all the way
From Africa, swooped past.
A buzzard mocked me, mewing overhead.
Then, on the wind of Spring.
I heard God crying in a curlew's call.

----<>----

BASHER B

We were a rotten class.
We felt it was our task
To bait new Masters,
Testing their resolve.

Then came a bearded man
With sandaled feet – oh, joy,
A lamb to sacrifice.
What sport – what fun we'd have.

*He played us* as a weasel plays a bird
Letting us gambol round behind his back
Pretending not to see our clumsy mimicry –
And then he pounced.

A clear transgressor
Seen, identified, called out
To stand before the class,
Dumb, insolent.

The Master reached
Deep in a pocket, found a knife
And gave it to the boy.
"Go to that privet bush outside," he said,
"And cut a stick.
A thick one, or a thin –
That is your only choice."

Now this was something new!
We waited breathless in that quiet room.
Dust drifted slow.
All sounds were muted, muffled, still.

The boy returned,
Shamefaced and apprehensive.
Swish – swish – swish
Game, set and match.

We sat in silence, listening
As 'Basher' read from Wordsworth –
Michael's tale,

>>>>

About a half-built sheepfold
High on Greenhead Ghyll.
I smelt the sheep's wool
And the bracken in the sun,
Felt lichen-crumbs on stones
And heard a skylark singing in that dusty room
That was no longer there.

I would not, could not, dare not,
Wanted not
To idle in this class.
Here was a Master
And a Man.

Some forty years of growth
Have passed since then.
The seeds he sowed,
Close to that cane,
Are coming to fruition –
Thanks to Basher B.

That Nom de Guerre
Is now a Chant d'amour.

----◇----

THE SECRET OF THE UNIVERSE    A song lyric

A bushman stood on the gleaming sand
On the shore of Walvis Bay
And he called to the whales that had swum past there
For a million years and a day
And he called to the whales that had swum past there
For a million years and a day.

For he was the last of the Bushman Race,
And little and old was he
But his people had failed in their sacred task
To pass on the Word from the Sea.

For the Whales had worked out the Hidden Theme
That had always eluded Man
And they wanted to share with the dominant race
The Universal Plan.                              >>>>

For they had learned to speak to the Bushman there
In whistles and grunts and clicks
A language common to Whales and Men –
Those little brown men with their sticks.

The Bushmen had tried to pass it on –
The World just would not hear
For what could a primitive savage know
That Science had not made clear?

On the twenty-first day a whale came
And swam in alone from the sea.
"You called me, my friend?" she said to the man.
The Last of the Whales was she.
"You called me, my friend?" she said to the man.
The Last of the Whales was she.

"That wonderful secret you told to us
Now is only here, in my head,
For the very last one of the Bushmen am I,
The rest of my kind are dead."

"And I am the last of the Whale kind,
We **must** find a way to pass on
The Secret known only to you and to me
Before you and I are gone."

"We have tried our best. I can do no more
For the World is deaf with conceit.
I'm weary now and I'm coughing blood.
Farewell, my Friend of the Sea."

The last of the Whales then turned away
To swim to the ocean vast
At the mouth of the bay – a Whaling Ship,
A red-sun flag at its mast.

The vultures pecked out the Bushman's eyes
Hyenas gnawed at his feet
And in Tokyo the gourmets dined
On the Last of the Whale's meat.

>>>>

The President strolled on the White House lawn
In a far off, mighty land
And talked with the head of NASA there
And learned of the space-flights planned.

"One day we'll fly off to worlds unknown
In that great expanse called 'Space'
And we'll look for intelligent beings there
And we'll build us a study base."

"We'd have to work their language out
And find some way to converse."
"Who knows," he quipped, "They might have found
The Secret of the Universe."
"Who knows," he quipped, "They might have found
The Secret of the Universe."

----◇----

## MY BROTHER TIM

My brother Tim makes poetry
But as machines.
Where I use words and rhymes,
Tim uses nuts and bolts,
Milled plastic blocks,
Electric motors,
Tiny gears and cogs
And PCB's, in combinations
Mystical to me,
A minor wordsmith.

I know I must refine my thoughts,
Condense, compress,
Make every word a working part
That makes a contribution to the whole.
If any poem I create
Is rough or clumsy, then
It just won't do for me.

Tim is the same.
Unspoiled by education
With a mind original in thought,
Bold in conception,
Delicate in detail,                                    >>>>

39

He creates machines
To change our money,
Handle coins or notes,
Do anything you ask.

If you've a need:
Mechanical, electrical
Or electronic – Tim
Can soon design and build
Some thing to do the job.

But not just any thing
To do it crudely.
What he will make will be
Compact and functional,
Contained within a stylish case,
The minimum of moving parts.

Quite probably a unique way
To use some Rule of Physics
In a way not done by anyone before.

The pride with which he shows it off
Is just as great as mine
When you allow me time
To read to you a poem I've composed.

I'd like to think we both create
Devices –
Each to fill a need
With Elegance.

----<>----

*Going through the mill*
*In some strange way -| releases*
*Creativity.*

----<>----

*Hot water bottles*
*Modest, unassuming things,*
*Comforters supreme.*

----<>----

## OUR SUGAR LOAF

A mountain stands behind Y Fenni town,
Not grand as mountains go, but very dear
To those who watch it change, white, green then brown,
To mark the changing seasons of the year.

We walk the beech-woods of Saint Mary's Vale,
The close-cropped grass above Llanwenarth Breast;
We stroll through stunted oaks, the Deri trail
Or take the Rholben ridge to reach the crest.

When pressures mount and life seems full of strain,
We climb this hill and breathe the sparkling air.
The peace and solitude there eases pain
And troubles shrink and often disappear.

If we must leave our lovely town to study, work or fight,
We know we're nearly home again when our Sugar Loaf's in sight.

*Y Fenni – The Welsh name for Abergavenny.*

----◇----

## CASTLE CADNO

Ten years ago, deep in the hills,
I found a castle, time-decayed,
Hidden amongst the birches and the pines,
So far from any human track,
It was forgotten and, praise be,
Unknown to Cadw and the National Trust.

The walls were crumbling,
Stones were loose and dangerous,
Adventure lurked up every spiral stair.
No concrete capping, handrails, hidden lights,
Only sad ghosts and romance lingered there.

A gang of jackdaws quarrelled in the long-cold stacks
And ringdoves coo'd from ivy-hidden nests,
Ferns filled the dungeons,
In the gloom, I heard the groans of English knights,
Glendower's unwilling guests.

>>>>

41

Where dark-eyed Morfydd once had barred her door
To thwart a prince's lust, I stood
And through her empty window
Watched a tired sun
Slide down behind Bryn Cadno.   In the dusk

A fieldmouse sat and preened its whiskers
Unafraid of me, a human form
More solid than the shapes it mostly saw
Walking those rooms at nightfall.

A breeze through mullioned windows blew
Chill, swirling dead leaves
Around the stone-flagged floor.
A silent owl wafted across the yard,
A stone fell from the tower wall.
My arms were nettles to my fingertips
My hair was bristles on a brush.
Not looking back, I left.

Beyond, a pair of pipistrelle
Weaving cats-cradles in between the trees
Ignored me, hurrying below.

Climbing the ridge, I slowed my pace
Then, looking back,
Sought out the tower above the trees.
The gleam of light I thought I saw
Could only be a chance reflection from the sky,
The scream, a vixen's call.

Until this day, I never told a soul
About my castle.

----◇----


E-BAY

I bought some glue on E-bay.
It cost a tidy sum.
The label on the parcel read –
'From Yorkshire – **E-bay Gum**.'

----◇----

## CHESIL BEACH

Today there is no wind.
The sea breathes deep and slow
Wet pebbles nudge each other, steal a kiss
And chuckle at their daring.
Portland lies, a lazy dog, facing the land,
Its nose between its paws.
The gulls, disconsolate
Sit bored along the ridge,
Peck at their toes.
Today there is no wind.

Today the wind is in the East.
Waves quarrel, run ashore, then
Change their minds, draw back.
The pebbles groan, clatter and tinkle,
Knock their neighbours, try to get away
Give up, surrender, nestle down.
Bright Portland sniffs the air, alert.
Gulls ride the waves off-shore and wait.
This won't last long.
Today the wind is in the East.

Today the wind is in the West.
Green breakers tower, check,
Hold their breath, crash down – to be devoured
By those that roar and chase behind.
Bruised pebbles scream and churn
Grinding their neighbours and themselves.
No pause – see, here's a plank – toss it ashore –
This stone is bigger – pass it on.  Now –
Pass it on along
Towards where wind-whipped Portland cowers,
Half-hidden by smoking spray.

Above, the gulls float joyously
White wings outstretched,
Tracing the contours of the living beach.
Alive, alive. Alive today.

Today the wind is in the West
And I am here, sea-salt upon my lips,
Alive.

----◇----

43

# A SHOT IN THE DARK

One night we stood, three boys and Da,
Under a starry sky, frost nipping our fingers.
Megan and Mam inside, knitting by the fire.
"Bloodthirsty lot, you." Mam said, but knowing the rats must die.
Our boots rustled the leaves.
We saw the hen-house, silent and dark, across the farmyard.
I felt the cord, taut as a bowstring.
Death at my fingertips.

That afternoon we'd driven a stake, lashed the Twelve-bore
And sighted, with infinite care, along the feed-trough.
The cord to the trigger now vibrated to my touch.
I pulled, gently.
Executioner. – Death by firing squad.

A blue flame stabbed at the night.
A charge of Eley Number Six raking the grain thieves.
The shot echoing around the silent hills.
A squeal of pain – dying.
Drowned by a cacophony of clucking
From hens awakened.

We ran across the yard, Da strode behind.
Light on. Not one or two – six dead  –
Our hopes exceeded.

Picking up corpses cautiously, by scaly tails,
We pitched the bodies callously
Into the midden.
The hens, unheeding, thinking it was day,
Pecked sleepily in the blood-spattered trough.
Petty gods, we reload. Lightning to strike twice.
It seemed so easy.
"Give them an hour."

Minutes passing slowly.
Clock ticking loudly.
Da winds it – not even Sunday!

>>>>

Once more, we rustled the leaves and pulled the cord of death.
No squeals this time.
Squawking and flapping wings.
"Dear God," said Da, hand on the switch.
"Your Mam will kill us."

Ten hens, caught by the darkness,
Had roosted on the trough edge,
Taking this charge.
Not a single rat to justify the carnage.
Downy fluff, small feathers, floated on air.
We stood, four gawping fools, dreading Mam's tongue.
"To market – full of pellets? There'd be talk in Chapel.
Those Price boys, shooting at chickens now."

That was ten days gone.
I'd murder for a slice of pork.

----◇----

INSIGNIFICANCE

At night I stand and watch the stars
So far away and yet so bright
To them, I'm insignificant,
A tiny speck of human life.
To them, I'm insignificant.

At night I stand and watch the stars
Great glowing balls of flaming gas
So far away and yet so bright
To them, I'm insignificant.

At night I stand and watch the stars
A billion miles away, or more,
So far away and yet so bright
To them, I'm insignificant.

At night I stand and watch the stars
So far away and yet so bright
I may be insignificant to them
But I am *here* and I am *me*.

>>>>

Yes! Here on tiny Earth I stand – Alive.
Here I find Joy and form it into Love
I relish Sensuality and seek The Truth
I think and plan and work and play,
Enjoy my family and friends
And every day I do the things that Men must do.

Perhaps, down here, I'm not so insignificant.

----<>----

*A secret pleasure –*
*Sitting on a toilet seat*
*Warm from one you love.*

----<>----

GYPSY MARY  (Raglan 1989)

I am my mother's son
Trusting, naive,
Many would say a fool.

Two months ago I sat
Worn out by care, my spirit drained.
I had been duped by men whose greed
Outweighed their honour.  Now
My brain was addled and my limbs were lead.
I then could see no way to clear my debts,
The future black, fear gripped my heart.

'Come on, Grandpa,' said little Jennifer, taking my hand,
'Let's walk up to the castle on the hill.'
My mother's eyes were twinkling in her little face.
Exhausted as I was from sleepless nights,
I rose, and hand in hand, we walked along the lane.

I hardly heard her chatter
As she pointed out the flowers and the birds,
Read all the road signs, spelling out each word.
Then, down by Barton Bridge
We met a gypsy woman and her little girl.

>>>>

46

The pair stood in my way
And would not step aside.
The woman stood there, forcing me
To look into her eyes.
'Would you buy from a gypsy, Sir?' she asked.
'Depends,' I said, 'on what she had to sell.'
(Expecting clothes-pegs for a silver coin.)
'Good luck and wealth,' she said.
I had to smile.

The child and Jennifer were playing by the bridge.
'I would buy that,' I said.
She took my hand, looked deep into my eyes.
'You are a kind man, Sir. Much hurt by trusting other men.'
Tears filled my eyes – How could she know?
She took two little charms and pressed them in my hand.

'In nine days' time your life will turn.
You have a wife who loves you more
Than you could know. She will stand by you.
Tell me, had you thought of leaving here?'
I said I wasn't – nothing further from my mind.
'You will,' she said, 'You will be moving soon.'
'You have a car?' she asked, 'A white one?'
'Yellow,' I said.
'I see you in a white one,' she replied.
'And you've had trouble with your back or legs?'
'My back,' I said.
'No more!' That was a statement.
So was this. 'You'll live to ninety three!'

I see a cheque here in your hand,' she said,
'Eight thousand pounds, before this month is out.'
How did she know the very sum I needed then
To get the Taxman off my back
And pay the mortgage up to date?
Was this telepathy – had she just read my mind?

I am my mother's son
Trusting, naive,
Many would say a fool.

>>>>

'My name is Mary, Sir.'
She looked into my eyes, 'What's yours?'
'Mike,' I replied.
'Well, Mike, take out your wallet,
Put into your hand, four banknotes.
Hold them tight.
The clever girl, *my* hand, not hers.
I did as I was bid.
'Now, Sir,' she asked, 'which would you rather have –
What I have seen for you, or what is in your hand?'

I smiled, for this was being neatly done.
Eight thousand pounds was here on offer,
Could I just turn it down for what was in my hand?

She saw the hesitation in my face.
'Blow twice into your hand,
And then give those to me.'
I did just that just that, feeling a fool
And glancing down the road.
No one about, thank God.
The children played together by the bridge.

'You are a kind man, Sir,' she said.
'You won't regret what you have done.
I'll meet you here again
At mid-day on the thirty-first of May.
If things are not as I have seen,
I'll give you back your money. Goodbye, Sir.'

Taking her child's hand
She went on up the road.
The child turned and waved to Jennifer.

I am my mother's son
Trusting, naive,
Many would say a fool.

And yet – the sun came out,
My step was lighter.
I could be a grandfather again
With little jokes for Jennifer.
We both enjoyed that walk.

>>>>

Nine days I waited
Wondering just what
Would happen on the ninth,
To change my life.

That day was just like any other – yet
I felt, as when the tide is low,
A sort of stillness, as it feels
Before the flow commences.

Next day I sensed a surge of strength
Lifting me off the mud-banks of despair.
Was this the flood which Shakespeare says
'Leads on to fortune?'

My mind was clear
I didn't give a damn about the Taxman
They could take the house, if it should come to that,
Jo would stand by me through it all!
But then – Eight thousand pounds would put it right.
Where from I could not guess,
But I believed it would be in my hand before the end of May
Mary had told me so!

I grew an inch a day.
No longer was my mind oppressed by fear
Or doubt about myself.
I worked from dawn to dusk
Six days a week.
I paced myself, taking a half-hour nap when needed
So that my mind stayed clear.
The problems that had loomed so large
Were now just minor challenges
Soon overcome.
Mere flotsam on the tide!

A mystic power filled me,
Reaching out
To those with whom I worked.
Was it emitted by those charms
I'd had from Mary down at Barton Bridge?

>>>>

Each day I waited for the cheque,
Watching each post. It never came, but
On the Thirty-first of May
I left the house at ten to twelve,
Sat on the bridge and waited.

Deep in my heart I knew she would not come,
And yet I hoped she would.
Not for my money back,
I had forgotton that – but just to thank her then.
That gypsy girl had given me
Hope, and an inner strength and understanding of myself.

Wherever you are, Mary,
'Thank you, Dear.'

I am my mother's son
Trusting, naive,
Many would say a fool.

----◇----

COCKLES AND ICE CREAM

Our Sunday school teacher was Ceinwen Jenkins.
In her thirties – or her forties.
"She'll not marry," Megan said.
"Too straightlaced, afraid to let her hair down."
In a bun, it was, black and shiny.
'Did she sleep in it, then?' I wondered.

Every Sunday, Ceinwen Jenkins would cross the valley,
With her prayer book, for taking 'school'.
Crossing the little plank bridge.
Every Sunday,
Me and my brothers would put a stone under the bridge end.

Every Sunday, Ceinwen Jenkins would cross the plank bridge.
Never learning!
Tipping into the water (only shallow).
Black shoes and stockings soaking, treading the pedals of the organ.
Singing "Jesus wants me for a sunbeam."

>>>>

Every August 'Outing' to the sea-side.
Can't go, though, till you're eleven.

My first outing was to Porth-y-Pyscod.
Me so excited. Never seen the sea.
Coach was waiting early morning.
Mam gave me five shillings for spending. So did Megan.

Children singing, led by Ceinwen,
"Jesus wants me" and "Bread of Heaven.
Smashing.
(Ate all of my sandwiches before we got as far as Brecon)

Lovely at the sea-side, paddling in the water.
Eating cockles and ice cream.

On the quayside, black baskets for catching lobsters.
Smelling of tar and fishes.
Eating cockles and ice cream.

Fishing boats in the harbour,
Their nets spread out and hanging
For drying in the sunshine.
Eating cockles and ice cream.

Back on the coach now.
Tired and sunburned.
Coach swaying on the corners.
Queasy.
Suddenly – cockles and ice cream, ice cream and cockles.

Ceinwen Jenkins helping,
Holding me, wiping my face with her hanky.
Lacy, smelling of lavender. I remember so clearly.
Hairpins dropping, her bun undoing.
Black hair silky round her shoulders.
Looked quite pretty.

"You sit by me, Huw," said Ceinwen,
Putting her arm around my shoulders.
Sleepy me – dozing, head on her bosoms.
Smelling of lavender – and mothballs.
Bosoms jerking. Was she crying?
Soon I was sleeping.                          >>>>

Every Sunday, my brothers would put a stone under the plank-bridge.
Every Sunday, I would go, after, and move it.
No wet shoes and stockings, now, in the chapel.
Ceinwen Jenkins never married.
Too straightlaced – afraid to let her hair down.

----◇----

THE TWO ESSENTIALS OF MODERN LIFE

When things stick together which should come apart
It's **WD 40** you need,
Just reach for the can and give it a spray
And whatever is binding – is freed.

That nut and that bolt that just won't unscrew,
Will drive even a saint to distraction
A squirt of this product will loosen them up
And lead to all-round satisfaction.

When tools go all rusty left out in the rain
And replacements are so damned expensive
Well, **WD 40** will keep them like new.
Against rust – it's your counter-offensive.

When things come apart which should stick together
And the pieces all fall to the ground
A roll of **Duct Tape** is all that you need –
An immediate solution is found.

A temporary fix or a permanent job –
**Duct Tape** will answer your prayers
It's done in a moment – just wrap a strip round –
I can tell you that nothing compares.

It sticks to most anything that you can name
Which it holds in a vice-like embrace
But when you release it – it comes away clean
And leaves a broad smile on your face.

If life's falling apart or you're stuck in a rut
And you start using words that are naughty
You could do much worse than to sort it all out
With **Duct Tape** and **WD 40**!

----◇----

## JOSEPH'S CHILD

I'm Joseph – just a carpenter
Come up to Bethlehem to pay my tax.
Last night my wife gave birth.
I should be glad, but no –
That baby lying over there,
He isn't mine.

I thought I heard a singing in the hills
An angel choir? It must have been a dream!
I was so tired from travelling and helping Mary through.
I should be glad, but no –
That baby lying over there,
He isn't mine.

The straw on which he lies is clean and sweet
Sweet as the oxen's breath that warms this cave
Better than at the over-crowded inn.
I should be glad, but no –
That baby lying over there,
He isn't mine.

The shepherds came with lambs. How did they know?
Is nothing private in these little towns?
Good fellows – honest working men like me.
I should be glad, but no –
That baby lying over there,
He isn't mine.

Three rich men came and left him presents –
Gold and frankincense and myrrh
As if he were a prince. This puzzles me.
I should be glad, but no –
That baby lying over there,
He isn't mine.

While Mary slept I went and looked into the child's eyes
Eager and bright – though with a sadness too.
His hand clasped round my finger – very tight.
And I was glad, so glad.

This baby, lying in my arms,
He's mine –
And yours –
And everyone's.

----◇----

53

# A NIGHT IN THE NAMIBIAN DESERT

The strangely silent night of Africa
Wrapped warm and dark about our little group.
A hundred yards away a petrol-driven power plant
Chugged and wheezed
Lighting our lonely camp.

The evening meal done, our guide stood up.
He stretched and said, 'When I turn that thing off
There'll be no artificial light for fifty miles around.'
He strode across the sand and threw the switch.

Eyes blinded by the sudden loss
We stumbled to our tents and,
As we fumbled with the ties,
High overhead a glowing canopy of light appeared.
Bright planets, distant stars and far-off galaxies
As closely packed, it seemed to me,
As were the grains of desert-sand beneath my feet.

Our galaxy, the Milky Way,
Threw a broad ribbon of even brighter light
Arching across the luminescent sky.

I pulled my bed out of the tent
And lay, snug in my sleeping bag,
Under the stars,
Looking up at this enchanting scene.

No insects chirped, no night birds called
There was no sense of prowling animals.
Silence was absolute.
Until my ears, or spirit, seeking for sound,
Tuned to the music of the stars.

A gentle hum, rising and falling,
As does the roar of some far-distant waterfall,
Reached deep into my soul.

I lay there all night long, awake,
Floating in space, as in a trance.

>>>>

Sometimes a shooting star flashed overhead
Random and unpredictable,
While glowing man-made satellites, precisely timed,
Slid steadily from east to west
Each locked within its rigid, pre-planned course.

At last dawn crept across the sky,
Washing away the fainter stars
And then the brighter ones –
The planets last to go.

Suddenly,
As is the way in Africa,
The sun was up.
Frost crystals on my sleeping bag,
Sparkled as if to imitate the vanished stars.

I closed my eyes and slept.

----◇----


THE DIVER

The diver got a message
That really got him thinking
The Captain signalled
'Come up quick –
The bloody ship is sinking!'

----◇----


DOORS

I always pull the door marked PUSH
And push the door marked PULL.
Am I alone in doing this?
Am I the only fool?

The other day I got upset,
In fact I got quite miffed.
I spent ten minutes puzzled by
A fancy door marked LIFT.

----◇----

# THE SONG OF THE DOLPHIN, *ELEGANCE OF ROCKALL* –
## (from the novel '*Dolphinsong*' 2000)

When I was born the sun-lit, sparkling Sea
Patterned the seabed, light delighting me.
Sun, Sea, companionship and joy were mine
Grace, beauty, love and peace would intertwine
As kelp-weed in a swirling current's flow.
Now – what is the life I know?

All I possess is here within my brain
I have no hands to grasp and hold and claim.
But human hands once cast a subtle net
Unseen, unheard, unechoeing and yet
Strong to ensnare, to capture and enslave
This spirit born for Sea-life, wind and wave.

For I was taught that Dolphins love all Men
And Men love us, but now I wonder when
Their arrogance and greed this concept killed –
Still whales and dolphins die. My soul is filled
With alien emotions. Fear and hate
Pollute my mind – a toxic stream in spate.

I am a symbol of all whales' plight
Captured or killed, not knowing how to fight.

Trapped here, I swim in circles and a hatred grows.
I yearn for freedom where the sea-wind blows.
Don't let a hate for Mankind poison me.
~Yegods~ and little fishes – set me free.

----◇----

*Do you remember*
*The Man from Del Monte?*
*I wanted his job.*

----◇----

*The ideal time*
*To plant a cherry tree is –*
*Twenty years ago.*

----◇----

56

# THE SONG OF THE DOLPHINE, *GRACE OF FAIR ISLE*
## (from the novel *'Dolphinsong'* 2000)

I, Fair Isle, call to thinking men –
See us for what we are.

Not competition for your fish
Not fools to entertain your young
Not handy hulks of oil and flesh
But creatures of intelligence
A Nation of our own,
Deserving something better
From our one-time friends
Who occupy dry portions of this planet
You call Earth
But which is mostly Sea.

We know that you have eyes to see
And ears to hear.
We know that you have brains to think,
We know imagination flourishes in men.
We hope that you have souls
To feel compassion, too.

Please use your hands to signal
STOP
And let us live.

See us for what we are:
A peaceful, gentle Nation of the Sea.

----◇----

*If you just knew all*
*Then you would understand all*
*Then you'd forgive all.*

----◇----

*It's the early bird*
*Who gets the worm, but the cheese*
*Feeds the second mouse.*

----◇----

APHRODITE

It was a hot day, and I mean HOT.
We don't get many in Wales.
My Four-Ten shotgun, new, light as it was, seemed heavy.
Lovely, though.
Stock polished, dark red mahogany.
The barrel – a kind of dark blue – sort of grape colour.
It was a present, now I was thirteen.
Made me feel a man.

Nothing to shoot at, too hot.
Rabbits underground, squirrels hiding in topmost branches.
Pigeons somewhere else.
Suddenly lonely.
Unusual for me.
Like being on my own, mostly.

Over the bridge movement, someone is coming.
Rhiannon from Trehelig.
Bit older than me, her.
Pretty she looks.
Blue skirt, white blouse, with flowers, Swiss-like.
Beginning to fill it too. Mysterious this, to boys.

"Hello, Rhiannon."
"Hello, Huw. Shooting?"
"Squirrels, shilling a tail. Tree rats, Da calls them."
"Hot today."
"Very."

Then me, greatly daring. "Fancy a walk, then."
"Where to?"
"Up by the stream."
Rhiannon nodded shyly.

Gun hidden under the bridge,
We walk by the water, sheep-paths through bracken.
Each bend a dipper, rising, skimming ahead and piping.
"Intruders."

>>>>

By the old sheep pen,
Now just boulders covered in lichen, Rhiannon stops.
"I fancy a paddle"
Shoes off, sitting on the bank, splashing and giggling.
Water so shallow.

"Let's make a dam," I said, not expecting a girl to want to.
Barefoot and lovely, skirt tucked in knicker-legs, Rhiannon wades in.
Passes me stones and handfuls of moss.
Water rising slowly.
Above our knees now,
Cold from springs deep in the mountain.

"Be able to swim soon," said Rhiannon,
Looking at me from under her lashes.
Fool as I was, I said, "No costume, no towel."
"Who's looking?" said Rhiannon,
Smiling sweet-like.

I remembered a picture,
'Aphrodite Rising from the Waves.'
I wandered – would she?
"I will if you will," I said, heart thumping.
"All right – but you first," she said,
Still smiling. Not wearing much anyway that day.
Soon off, and me in the water.
Cold but lovely.

"Come on then," I called.
"In a minute.
Look at that Polly Wagtail."
It was perched on a boulder, bobbing and curtseying,
Like we were royal.

I splashed about, pretending to be swimming, waiting.
Rhiannon sat there, watching.
"Come on then," I called.
"Changed my mind now," she said,
Looking at the wagtail forwards
But watching me sideways.

>>>>

Silly I felt then, splashing to show I didn't care.
Chilling now, in the water.
Got to come out sometime; might as well be now.
Standing up, feet numb, I stumble on stones,
Climb out, not looking at Rhiannon
But knowing she is watching me.
I dressed, still wet.

"You promised," I said, disappointed.
She still looked lovely.
"I was lying then," she said.
'Truthful, at least,' I thought.
'A truthful liar.'
I smiled at that and the sun seemed warm again.

Rhiannon leading, we walked through the bracken
Down to where the bridge was.
Not smiling now, she said, "I'm sorry, Huw. I had to.
No brothers, see."
That smile again.
Under the bridge to get the gun.
Back up, she's gone.

Rhiannon's married now –. Mrs Dai Parry.
Three children.

I see her sometimes in the market.
 She smiles then and looks at me sideways.
I like that.

Aphrodite.

----◇----

*Fishing is enjoyed*
*More by anglers than by fish,*
*Even less by worms.*

----◇----

*I have a pet newt.*
*I call him "Tiny". For why?*
*Because he is My Newt.*

----◇----

## THE LOST SONG OF TEMBO JAY
(from the novel *God's Elephants, 2006)*

Be kind, be gentle, and be fair
Find Joy and turn it into Love
Create enough for all to share.

When life is more than you can bear
Seek Joy and turn it into Love
Be kind, be gentle, and be fair.

When others mock – brace up and dare
They do not know the Joy of Love
Create enough for all to share.

Don't be afraid – show that you care
Teach how to turn that Joy to Love
Be kind, be gentle, and be fair.

If no one listens – don't despair
Just practise turning Joy to Love
Create enough for all to share.

The simple truth will soon be clear
That **all** we need is Joy and Love
Create enough for all to share
Be kind, be gentle, and be fair.

----◇--

*Evocative sound*
*Heard on sun dappled mountains,*
*A curlew calling.*

----◇----

*A girl on a swing.*
*Her skirt flying in the wind.*
*Such joy on her face.*

----◇----

THE WHALE'S SONG
(From the novel *God's Elephants. 2006*)

In the dim and distant ages
This our planet was quite lifeless.
Came a time when it was ready
Ready like a flower open,
Craving for a speck of pollen.

Floating in from where we know not
Came a drift of cosmic pollen
Carrying the sacred Life-force
To this silent, waiting planet.

Like the flower gaining pollen
Earth responded to this Life-force.
Simple plants and simple creatures
Flourished here in great abundance
Making from this sterile body
Something more than rocks and water.

As time passed these plants and creatures
Grew more complex, found their places
Leading to a wondrous richness
Making up the world around us.

On the way a million, million
Plants and creatures formed and flourished
Failed and perished, died and vanished.
Others – fitter, stronger, better,
For the role that needed playing
Took their places in this complex
Web of interactive life-forms.

At some point, a mystic union
Of these plants and other creatures,
With the earth and rocks and water
Formed a being whales call 'Gaia'
Mother-being of our planet.

>>>>

Gaia, like a mother whale,
Knew the Joy of Procreation
Knew her role, to care and nourish.
But another force was needed
With intelligence and forethought
Powered by Love – she named him 'Mana'.

Gaia chose from all her creatures
Four to serve our planet's interests
Four to give it thought and focus
Four to save it from destruction.

From the oceans she chose whales
Great in body, great in wisdom
With a brain that could develop
Play a part in forming Mana.

As a balance, she chose dolphins
Smaller, joyful, fond of playing
Loving freedom, kind and caring
Dolphins would be good for Mana.

Greatest on the land were tembos                    [elephants]
Like the whales, great in wisdom
Storing in their tusks the Loving
Mana needed for his workings.

Lastly, Gaia chose the humans
Smaller, joyful, fond of playing
Loving freedom, kind and caring
Humans would be good for Mana.

Whales, dolphins, tembos, humans
All were granted 'beings' greater
Than their bodies, blood and brains were.
Call these 'beings' – souls or spirits,
Hallowing the chosen foursome.

All the myriad other life-forms
Fill the needs of whales and dolphins,
Feed the tembos and the humans
So they can devote their lives to
Service for the good of Mana.

>>>>

Link these spirits round the planet
Link the spirits of the foursome
Link the whales and the dolphins
With the tembos and the humans
Call this combined spirit – Mana.

Think of Gaia as our mother
Caring for the plants and creatures.
Think of Mana as our father
Planning for our planet's future
Seeing what needs doing.      Only –
With no hands or trunks or flippers
He needs US to do what's needed.

His the vision, ours the labour
Without Mana, we are nothing
Without us, he's nothing either
Mana needs us – we need Mana.

We need food to fill our bellies,
Give us strength to live and flourish,
Make more whales, dolphins, tembos
Make more humans – all are needed
To ensure that Mana lives on.

Our role is serving Mana
Seeking Joy in all around us
Seeking Joy and with it forming
Love, to power the work of Mana.

It's from Joy that Love emerges
Transmuted by our souls and spirits
Joy – to Love  Our gift to Mana.
He needs Love as we need fishes,
Meat or plants to fill our bellies.
It is Joy that we must cherish
Turn to Love to nourish Mana.

If we choose to take what's offered,
Giving nothing, being greedy,
Never giving Love to Mana,
Thinking that our selfish comforts
Justify our whole existence,
We will grow away from Mana.                    >>>>

64

Then our lives will be so empty
We can't ever link with Mana.
Arrogance and fear will fill us
Fear of loss and Fear of dying.
In the hearts and souls of whales
In the hearts and souls of dolphins
In the hearts and souls of tembos
In the hearts and souls of humans.

Real Love and real caring
Take away these Fears forever.

Listen to the voice within you
That is Mana, speaking softly
Saying what you should be doing
Sometimes hard and sometimes easy.
Don't ignore that voice within you
Or Mana's plans can't reach fruition.

Mana needs the Love we give him,
Formed from Joy and care for others
For Love is the magic power
The Force that links us all together.

Here's the wonder, here's the beauty
Here's the honour, here's the duty
We can all be part of Mana.

We will all be part of Mana
If we share the Love within us
Love that Mana needs to function
To ensure our planet's future
As a place of Truth and Beauty,
Harmony and Peace – for ever.

----◇----

*We are so wise  – But*
*Whales, dolphins and elephants*
*All have bigger brains*

----◇----

## LETTING GO

Dementia is the cruellest thing
And, when it took my wife,
My love for more than sixty years,
My family and friends all said
'It's for the best, she will not suffer now.
You must let go, move on.'

My daughters, with great sensitivity,
Spirited away her clothes, her shoes, her scarves
And all the wide-brimmed hats
She wore so stunningly at weddings in the family.

My son and my four lovely girls
Shared out her jewellery and all the little things
That held fond memories for them.

For me, I knew I must 'let go, move on.'
A photo of a smiling girl
Taken when she was just sixteen,
Was all I needed then.

But there was something else so personal
That bothered me – her toothbrush
In the bathroom, next to mine.
Three times I dropped it in the bin.
Three times I took it out
Not really knowing why.

Then came the day when my old toothbrush,
Bristles all awry,
Looking like some bedraggled mini-porcupine,
No longer did its job.
Definitely time to buy myself another  –
The old one for the bin.

And then I knew what I must do.
Into the bin it went,
But not alone.

Two toothbrushes, together now,
Would make the one-way journey

>>>>

Sort of hand in hand,
To some far land-fill site
And lie there, side by side,
For ever and a day.

And now I could let go, move on.

----◇----

MIXED POSIES

In Cwm Cadno
The old houses on the hillside were all ruins
Long deserted.
Just stone walls covered in mosses and lichen.
Fireplaces empty,
Ivy on the chimneys,
Rooms full of nettles.
No one remembered who lived there.
But every springtime
The gardens were full of flowers –
Snowdrops, primroses and daffys.
Sometimes a lily.
In one garden a rose grew, defiant.

Mam and Megan would pick the flowers for market,
In bunches of a dozen.

Mam made something special for the Market.
"Mixed Posies" she called them.
Different flowers from the gardens
And the meadows
Depending on the season.

Each posy a mass of colour
Fragrant from violets, budding roses
Or stocks, sweet scented.
Only sixpence for a posy.
Townsfolk loved them.

Mam is gone now.
But sometimes in the Market
I remember "Mixed Posies"
And Mam.

----◇----

## SCATTER MY ASHES HERE

Scatter my ashes *here* – on Dorset's Chesil Beach
This vast and awesome icon of my youth
My 'Living Beach', my 'Abacus of God'.
Here I can feel the wave-churned pebbles grind
And taste the salt-spray flying on the wind.

But No! – I would be less than nothing *here*
Devoured and lost in its immensity.
And so – *Not here* – This cannot be my resting place!

Scatter my ashes *here* – beside this pool so blue
Where heather-bells and resin scent the air
Where wood-ants, deer and squirrels spend their lives
With distant views of Brownsea and the coast.

But No! – Although I've always loved this spot
It is a place to visit – not to stay
Here I'd be trodden underfoot
And trampled in the sun-baked Purbeck clay.
And so – *Not here* – The ants might eat me here!

Scatter my ashes *here* – upon Llangattock's Humpy Bog
Held in this mountain's sheltering hand,
Close by the cells of long-dead holy men.
Here falcons soar and circle overhead
And frog-voiced ravens haunt the tree-clad cliffs.
Here springs flow clear and sweet from rock-lined pools
And hawthorns thrive, despite shoot-nibbling sheep.

But No! – Although this is a peaceful place
Few people come – I would be lonely *here*
And winter freezes hard the barren peat.
And so – *Not here* – For how I hate the cold

Scatter my ashes *here* – upon the Sugar Loaf.
This ever-changing backdrop to my town,
Seen from far off, it says I'll soon be home.

>>>>

Here I came many times when I was young,
Blood pounding from the vigour of the climb –
Loving the views – from Pen-y-Fan to Malvern's hills –
Thrilled by the melancholy curlews' calls.

But No! – I'll have no eyes to see these views,
No pulse to race from the exertion of the climb,
No ears to hear the plaintive curlew's cry,
And so – *Not here* – I would be wasted here!

Scatter my ashes *here* – beneath this weeping birch.
Betula Pendula – its Latin name
Declaiming dignity and graceful form.
It does not weep for me – but for the world
Drawing my love out daily through my window-pane
And throwing it upon the eager wind
And – so I like to think – to those who need love most.
Yes – Spread my ashes *here* upon the ground
Where lively children play at hide-and-seek

Where I can sense the Cibi flowing near.
Here what is left of me, beneath this tree,
Will sink into the soil to nourish roots,
Be drawn each Spring by sugar-laden sap
Up, up to where the wind-tossed, cheerful jackdaws play
Where, with the blesséd sunlight's magic kiss,
The nascent buds all turn to dainty leaves
To throw more love out to a needful world.
So I will live again, and yet again.
*This* is the place – *This* is the very place –
I will be happy here – and useful too!

----◇---

*Seek Joy in your life.*
*Learn to change this into Love*
*And share it around.*

----◇---

69

## NEARLY THERE

"Daddy. Are we nearly there?" I asked.
"Not far to go now," he replied.
But when he passed around the bag of sweets,
I knew it was a fib.
I think I slept a bit.

It's when I saw the cliff-top trees,
Swept backwards by the wind,
And smelt the seaweed washed up on the beach,
I knew that we *were* nearly there.

"Doctor. Have I long to live?" I asked.
"Oh, years and years," he said.
But when he passed to me the half-filled glass,
I knew it was a fib.
I think I slept a bit.

Once more I see the cliff-top trees,
Swept backwards by the wind.
Once more I smell the seaweed washed up on the beach
So now I know once more that I *am* nearly there.

---◇---


*A wild swan, dying*
*(So the legend tells) will sing*
*One last sweet lament.*


*Does Life end with Death?*
*Many believe not. One day*
*All of us will know!*

----◇----

## NOW AND THEN
(In Memoriam)

Now
When you see a squirrel on a branch
Hear pigeons coo, woodpeckers drum,
Just pause and say
"He loved all this"

Now
When you see cloud-shadows slide across a sunlit hill
Feel waves crash on a pebble beach
Look around and say
"How he loved that"

Now
When you walk beside a mountain stream
Or watch a river glide past time-smoothed stones
Toss in a twig and say
"He would swim here."

Now
When you see a reed-mace tall
Its head in sun, its roots in glorious mud
Laugh at a memory and say
"He would be that."

Then
If you should hear a lonely curlew's cry
Drift, bubbling, down the wind
Listen and say
"Does anyone remember Whatsisname?"

----◇----

THE END
(or perhaps not!)

NOVEMBER WOOD.
By Barbara Anne Knight.

A butterfly lost in bleak November,
Spins like torn paper.
Radiance dimmed by Autumn fog.
Ghostly, fluttering prisoner
Of the knife-edged wind,
It looks for any shelter, warm and safe
To while away the winter.

But it looks in vain.
Relentless Nature will not hold her breath
For one late flying traveller
To find a home.
Fragile as happiness,
It floats down through the trees,
Carelessly, it drifts to certain death.

----◇----

**Barbara Anne Knight   1944 – 2017**

----◇----